My favourite colour's purple now

Nadia Khan

BookLeaf Publishing

Presentation by *BookLeaf Publishing*

Web: www.bookleafpub.com

E-mail: info@bookleafpub.com

ISBN: 9789357611336

First edition 2022

DEDICATION

To those whose souls drip with passion, whose spirit is ignited with a yearning to travel beyond the horizon, for those of you who are walking, breathing poetry.

This is for you.

I love you.

ACKNOWLEDGEMENT

To those of you who feel like poetry, thank you. Thank you to my beautiful mother, who has taught me to notice the veins in leaves and reminded me to stop and appreciate the wind. Thank you Mum, for being the rock to my seaweed, my motivation and my inspiration. To my father, thank you for supporting me with my spontaneous decisions and encouraging my wacky self. To my brother, Daniel, thank you for giving me bears when I cry, and for your reluctant hugs (they mean a lot). To C, thank you for being you, for experiencing the universe with open arms and persevering; you mean so much to me. Thank you to my literature teacher, for allowing me to express myself and encouraging my complete love for literature and expressionism. My poetry interweaves fragments of each of you, your dreams and also, bits of the universe, for you to devour.
I must also thank you, you who has picked up my anthology, one that encapsulates both my heart and soul, which now radiate freely at your finger tips.
You are endless. Why be the sailor who tells the story, when you can be the pirate that lived it?
Thank you so incredibly much.

Sincerely, I thank you.
Much love, Nadia

PREFACE

Interwoven delicately within these pages is the restless energy of my soul, the passion of my fingertips, the vulnerability of my heart and the intricate labyrinth of a yearning mind.
These formations of ink that you now caress, are haunted by the echoes of a shattered heart, a whisper of a once cowering, intimidated soul, reminiscing last hugs and gentle smiles, under the nakedness of the sky.
These very whispers, you may come to find, may appear as no stranger to you; you may encounter familiarity within my words, traces of your sleepless nights, lingering conversations exchanged with one your heart once built a home in...
Alternatively, you may find that, much like a phoenix, you are reborn from these pages. What were once quiet whispers, announce your presence with the roar of a lion. You may find your ears filling with the laughter of a loved one, or that your eyes learn to graciously accept the beauty of yourself.
I trust you to hold my thoughts, to absorb special pieces of my soul that you too, may find connection and familiarity in. My heart is in your hands now. Whilst some may have not

done so to you, please handle it with care, and in turn, I will cradle yours in mine.

Always and Forever

You make something your home
Moreover, you make someone your home.
You build the walls from their hugs
The floor from their kisses.
The sweet aroma mocks their scent. The ceiling, crafted from their tender touch. This type of home can take mere days to build… maybe a year… or maybe two. It takes resilience and trust. It takes many good days and sometimes, an even larger amount of bad days. But sometimes, you may find, the house may begin to erode. Those foundations you thought to be so strong, begin to faulter. The songs whispering around the walls can decay, from a sweet melody, to the suffocating shrieks of lament. Those walls can begin to crumble. And one day, you may find yourselves sitting on the grass, amidst the fallen love. That broken love. How can something that was so beautiful, end? We put in so much effort. So many days. So many hours. So many laughs. So many tears. So much strength. It took us almost two years to build our house. We'd painted the walls every colour of the rainbow. Stuck our future on the ceilings. Polished the floorboards and filled our closets with love and personality. We tucked away the

lies and the voices, banishing them underneath the carpet, embellishing any imperfections within the tiles, in golden swirls. Overtime, the voices grew louder and the forbidden pile under the carpet grew, and woosh. The tiles cracked, and an ocean of decay that once crept around the house's corners, crashed through to every room of the house; strangling amongst it, our hundreds of yearning embraces, lost promises of eternity, the family dinners, your mother's cooking…
The pain starts to seep through. The strength of those emotions starts to knock over our hard work. Hard work built by individuals so young and yet, so recklessly and unforgivably in love.
Until eventually, all that's left is the memories of the house and the pictures that were placed so delicately and dangerously inside.
I guess it will be okay.
We will build new houses (but I'll always keep a fragment or two from ours).

P.S. I added a chain to our old key and wear it around my neck. I hope that's okay?

The glint in your eye

Must one solidify that which is desirable, for it
to truly exist?
To acknowledge the truths behind the extent of
that which I yearn for, must it become engraved?
Is it a requirement that, for something to be
recognised, I must etch it so deeply into my skin,
forcing a potentially temporary glint, into one
promising the unwavering illusion of
immortality?

- I just turned 18. Is this not what I'm supposed
to be doing?

Endearment

The corners of their lips arose, and I guess 'time stopped'
a pause mimicking the sun's morning routine.

My screen brightened, and under the banner echoing your name, were the words,
'how're you doing?'

That's it.
I must love them.

Those corners softened and discovered the corners of my lips,
because that's what we're here to do...
right?

Your fingertips brushed my waist.
There's no way that this is just lust.

No banner appeared on my screen last night.
Are you mad at me?
If so, that's okay!
I was the one who didn't kiss you hard enough after all...

A friend came crying to me.

That couple is plagued by an unbelievably venomous relationship.

Thank God I'm not in one.

- I guess you're untouched too, right?

Once more? I won't ask again.

Here, hold my clothes.
We'll toss them onto the floor and pray the guilt seeps through into the fibres of your carpet.
Here, caress my body.
It matters not who you are, just that I possess the bittersweet, mendacious reprieve that a body can fleetingly gift me.
Here, I'll stay with you throughout the night.
I will leave tomorrow, as my subconscious whispers the echoes of my torment throughout your halls, trailing lament through the air, and interweaving abandonment, amidst the sharp fangs of your duvet.

Unintentional Duplicity

I remember the carousel dearly, for my
memories of it are fond.
Oh, how it was picturesque, solidified and
vibrant amongst the stark grey.
How it shall forever remain unscathed, confident
in its status; I thought.
Thought wrong I must have.
It was but a subconscious brush against my
shoulder and a careless whisper in my ear that
feebly yearned to caution, all but at the mere age
of seven.
Seven. An age revelled in innocence; dipped in
reality and dowsed in vulnerability.
Yet all that lingered of the feeble, cautionary
attempts was the magic that emanated from the
carousel's base.
It had six... no, seven radiant horses.
Were they ponies?
Unicorns?
No... Horses. They were horses.
Horses dipped in mistruths and drenched
marvellously in carefully altered fabrications.

It didn't matter what animals they were; I could never quite bring myself to get off anyway, and break away from the spinning.

My favourite colour's purple now

my favourite colour's purple now,
not blue, nor pink or yellow.
how could it be blue, when our tender affections
were exchanged under it?
it could never be pink, too many of your gifts
were the sweet colour of a watermelon, and your
cheek would illuminate that colour, when i
kissed it.
i suppose it could never be yellow; that's the pale
shade of the sand from our day at the beach,
where i created failed sand tunnels, as your arms
lay wrapped around me.
they could never be my favourite colours. not
again.
so i changed it.
i tried to change it.
i try to change it.
yet the corners of my mouth rise and my eyes
form a spark at the blues, pinks and yellows at
the falling of the day; still, i reiterate, my
favourite colour's purple now.
please remember that.

They try to tell me I saw a ghost

It is all too accepted that with separation, fragments are formed.
Some end up with these fragments - others do not.
I suppose I was bittersweetly cursed with an eternal melancholy of not the heart, but sight itself.
Interwoven within the veins of the saturated leaves, dotted amongst the sky and tangled within the rich vines submerging the trunks, I saw you. You hid behind the trees, camouflaged against the depths of the forest.
Light illuminated.
You were happy, whistling the tune of your favourite song, as your sweet tune twisted to corruption in my ears; this was seemingly before you whistled to a body whom lacked the mere knowledge of the song you so effervescently sang.

Compatibility

Are we truly incompatible?
Please don't say that we are.
I know our minds are wired differently and because of that, harm can be unintentionally inflicted.
Through no fault of your own, I find myself regretfully with an aching heart.
Yet, engulfed by your obliviousness and haunted by wishful expectations, I will not allow us to be irreconcilable.
Despite the voices dowsed in concern, whom caution me repeatedly, I shall not hear that we are incompatible.
Please do not tell me that we will be eternally incompatible.

I'll see you when I see you, and I'm finally okay with that

Our last days are lurking in the shadows.
Our last ever bell-ringing stings my thoughts
that lay in an anxious slumber in the dark and
yet,
your freedom no longer obscures my hopes of
flourishing.
In my visions of your forthcoming opportunities,
the clouds encapsulating four years of
consequential lament have finally found solace
in our silence.

Even the title lingers like an afterthought.

You're the same as every other one of my stories.
You possess a beginning, a half-written middle
and a painful absence of any ending.
I keep you in the depths of my closet, lying
amongst the other ghosts, wishes, whispers,
afterthoughts and memories of an existence
enchanted with sorrowful romance and
utterly-joyous melancholy.
There you lie amidst the other shadows of lost
loves and failed expectations as I weep, too
afraid to form any finalisations, yet too shaken
to begin another page.

Desperation.

Napkin's crumpled on the table.
Glass shatters.
Glasses wonky.
The kettle squeals.
Paper towel sprawled on the floor.
Bitter silence.
The glass tips.

The Climb.

The sun's death threatened us once again, as midnight's creature's arose in a shallow attempt to lighten the heavy evening. Yet, their jagged wings thrashed with such melancholy, that if you were to allow the softening of your eyes and dismiss any permittance of the whispers blowing you away, you may hear the roaring of passionate crowds balancing in the horizon; echoing just enough for you to see the glowing silhouettes of tales old, joyously bound to the stadium seats.

The moon never did tell me to stop.

You barricaded the echoes of your laughter within my bedroom walls and at night time, I become so desperate for silence that I try to break it down.

Phenomena

Much like the sea gloated to the moon,
idealising the wishful responsibility to create her
waves, you unregretfully tainted my priorities.
Many alterations lingering with will can only be
described as the phenomenon, known as love.

tell me you love me, before the last leaf falls.

please?

p.s. you are the horizon i would chase forever.

Longing

She was the stars and I,
the sea.
Always near by,
yet never destined to be.

her waves are getting bigger

maybe the moon is weighed down by our
troubles.
her craters, formed by unnecessary grief.
her shadows, an attempt at protection from our
lament.

I found you again, in another dimension

Closed eyes and an outwardly-silent mind.
The aftermath of a splendid endeavour.
Eyes open and I mourn echoes of utter beauty
that fleeted my thoughts all too rapidly.
Yet as my mouth fell, that which I mourned
poured out, and flew.
I caught it quickly, trapping my second chance
within the scraps of a napkin, daring to not let it
go again.

Read this not, for I wish not to burden you with my admiration.

Where others curled inwards, you encapsulated nothing but joy, as the rain poured down and ethereal projections encircled us.
In the flashing lights, I found myself unregretfully bursting with bubbles of child-like glee, as your infatuation for life radiated from your movements.
Your tears rolled down your cheeks and onto the grass and I smiled. You're just like me, I thought. Completely overcome by the sheer magic encapsulated by the universe, fully surrendering to each awakening as they arise.

P.S I love that you love life.

untouched steel. be proud of you.

when something horrific happens,
it is but a social normality, to steer away.
in the midst of a heart, one may find the prevalence of an absent desire to return to the originality of the pain's initiation.
it is because of this that you whispered to me, that for the rest of her life, she truly may never return to your home, despite adoring it dearly.
he has walked through these doors, he has loved all around the dining room table and his hands have possessed much of the beloved objects in the shed.
oh, how he loved those possessions. his possessions. in the shed.
for they are in the shed now and he is no longer there for me to visually witness walking through those doors and thus, i shall not return there. not due to any distaste for the home of my loved ones, but because, i cannot bear it.

p.s. i saw her face on social media... did she succeed in a return?

p.p.s. we are all so proud of her

The price of poetry

it aches, and it claws and it tears.
'let me out, I need to breathe,' it cries.

and so, i compulsively set it free, desperately
harnessing whatever is nearby.

p.s. freedom has been attained through napkins,
scraps of paper, my leg, my arm, my phone, my
hand/s, my exam papers, canvases, leaves, and
more...

p.p.s. i wouldn't have it any other way.

www.ingramcontent.com/pod-product-compliance
Lightning Source LLC
Chambersburg PA
CBHW062205160726
48282CB00027B/1002
* 9 7 8 9 3 5 7 6 1 1 3 3 6 *